THE CHICAGO WHITE SOX

Sloan MacRae

PowerKiDS press™

New York

Published in 2012 by The Rosen Publishing Group, Inc.
29 East 21st Street, New York, NY 10010

First Edition

Editor: Amelie von Zumbusch
Book Design: Greg Tucker
Layout Design: Ashley Drago

Photo Credits: Cover (background), pp. 7, 22 (left) David E. Klutho/Sports Illustrated/Getty Images; cover (Nellie Fox), p. 15 Francis Miller/Time & Life Pictures/Getty Images; cover (Frank Thomas), p. 17 Jonathan Daniel/Allsport USA/Getty Images; cover (Alexei Ramírez) Ronald C. Modra/Sports Imagery/Getty Images; p. 5 Ron Vesely/MLB Photos via Getty Images; pp. 9, 13 Mark Rucker/Transcendental Graphics/Getty Images; p. 11 New York Daily News Archive via Getty Images; pp. 19, 22 (right) John Grieshop/MLB Photos via Getty Images; p. 21 Scott Boehm/Getty Images; p. 22 (center) Hulton Archive/Getty Images.

Library of Congress Cataloging-in-Publication Data

MacRae, Sloan.
 The Chicago White Sox / by Sloan MacRae. — 1st ed.
    p. cm. — (America's greatest teams)
 Includes index.
 ISBN 978-1-4488-5011-2 (library binding) — ISBN 978-1-4488-5155-3 (pbk.) — ISBN 978-1-4488-5156-0 (6-pack)
 1. Chicago White Sox (Baseball team)—History. I. Title.
 GV875.C58M33 2012
 796.357'640977311—dc22

                                        2011002671

Manufactured in the United States of America

CPSIA Compliance Information: Batch #WS11PK: For Further Information contact Rosen Publishing, New York, New York at 1-800-237-9932

CONTENTS

GHOSTS OF THE PAST

The Chicago White Sox have sometimes stood for everything that is good about American sports. At other times, they have stood for everything that is bad. At one point, the White Sox were the most hated team in America. People had good reason to be angry with them. The White Sox had been among the best teams in the history of **Major League Baseball**. They wound up almost destroying the sport, though.

Today the White Sox are proof that hard work can make up for the mistakes of the past. They fought back to become one of baseball's best teams. They won back the hearts of many fans, too.

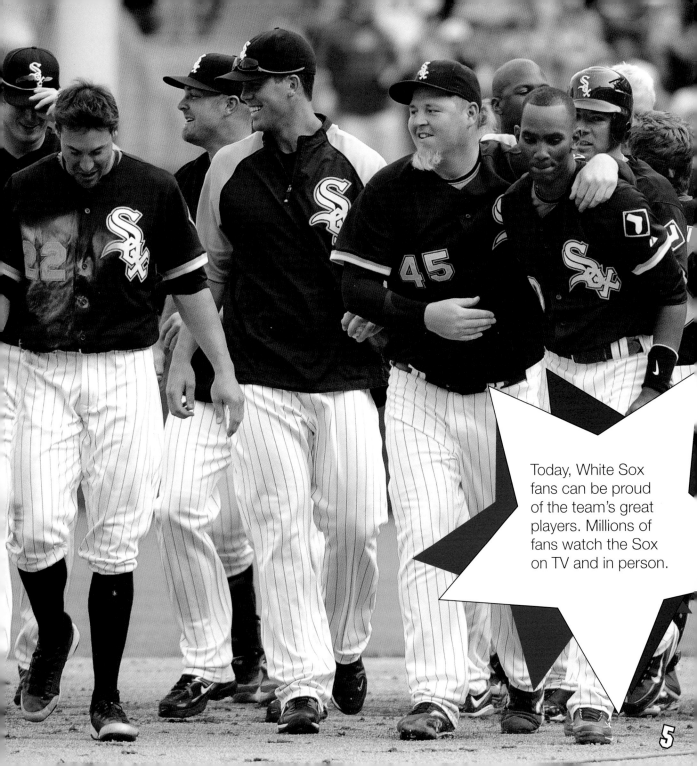

Today, White Sox fans can be proud of the team's great players. Millions of fans watch the Sox on TV and in person.

THOSE SOCKS DON'T LOOK WHITE

The White Sox play in Chicago, Illinois. Their **stadium** is called U.S. Cellular Field. It stands in a part of the city called the South Side. The team's colors are black, gray, and white. Their **logo** shows the word "SOX" in either black or white letters. The White Sox get their name for wearing white socks. However, at first look, it seems their socks are black! This is because they often wear black **stirrups** over their white socks.

The White Sox are not the only baseball team in their town. The Chicago Cubs are another great team. They are big **rivals** of the White Sox.

U.S. Cellular Field got its name in 2003. Before that, it was called Comiskey Park. The stadium replaced an earlier stadium that was also called Comiskey Park.

THE HITLESS WONDERS

The White Sox were not always based in Chicago. A former baseball player named Charles Comiskey bought a team from Sioux City, Iowa, in 1894. He moved them to St. Paul, Minnesota, in 1895. In 1900, he moved them to Chicago. There the team became known as the White Stockings. This was later changed to the White Sox.

In Chicago, Comiskey started putting together one of the best teams in baseball. The 1906 White Sox were nicknamed the Hitless Wonders. They won games even without having good batters. Excellent **pitching** and **defense** helped the Hitless Wonders beat the Chicago Cubs in the **World Series**.

Ed Walsh was a star pitcher for the White Sox during the 1900s and 1910s. He was one of the pitchers who earned the 1906 team their nickname.

9

THE BLACK SOX

The White Sox were even better in 1917, when players like Shoeless Joe Jackson and Eddie Cicotte led the team to beat the New York Giants in the World Series. White Sox fans believed their team would remain the best in baseball. No one saw what was coming next.

The White Sox reached the World Series again in 1919. This time they faced the Cincinnati Reds, but they lost. The problem was that they lost on purpose. Several White Sox players received money for letting the Reds win. Eight players were banned from Major League Baseball for life. They were called the Black Sox.

Shoeless Joe Jackson (right) was one of the players who was banned for life. Before that, he had been one of the team's best players.

BAD LUCK

The Black Sox were terrible for the game of baseball. Many fans stopped following the sport. They believed it was fixed.

The White Sox also started losing because their best players had been kicked off the team. They went from being baseball's best team to its worst team. They would remain at the bottom for about 30 years. Not even star players such as Luke Appling and Ted Lyons could break the team's bad luck. Some fans thought that the team was cursed for throwing the World Series back in 1919. Many people turned their backs on the White Sox and became fans of the Cubs instead.

Luke Appling played for the White Sox between 1930 and 1950. He was one of the team's best hitters during those years.

GO-GO

Nellie Fox helped turn things around for the White Sox in 1959. He was a great player with both his bat and his glove. In fact, in 1959, Fox was voted the American **League** most valuable player, or MVP. This means he did more to help his team than any other player. Fans began to call the team the Go-Go White Sox because they played with speed. The Go-Go White Sox reached the 1959 World Series. However, they lost to the Los Angeles Dodgers.

The Sox continued to play well in the 1960s. They failed to win any **championships**, though. The 1977 team had great batters called the South Side Hitmen.

Nellie Fox played for the White Sox from 1950 to 1963. He played second base for the team.

ALMOST THERE

Hitting continued to be an important part of South Side baseball. Tony La Russa became the White Sox's **manager** in 1979. He helped bring great hitters like Carlton Fisk to the team. The Sox got a new **shortstop** named Ozzie Guillén in 1985. Fans did not know it yet, but Guillén would be very important to the history of their team.

Star pitcher Jack McDowell won the American League Cy Young Award in 1993. This is given to the very best pitcher in baseball. The Sox enjoyed one of their best seasons ever in 1994. Then, baseball players went on **strike** and the season ended. Chicago's bad luck continued.

Frank Thomas was a star for the White Sox in the 1990s. He played first base and was a designated hitter. This is the hitter who hits in place of the pitcher.

17

THE RETURN OF OZZIE

The former White Sox star Guillén came back to the team in 2004. This time he was not a player. He was the manager.

Guillén knew that he could get his team back to the World Series. In 2005, he did just that. The **slugger** Jermaine Dye led the White Sox to one of the biggest championship wins in baseball history. The Sox did not just beat the Houston Astros. They also won every game in the series! This is called a sweep. At long last, the White Sox had turned their luck around. It was the team's first championship since 1917.

Here, White Sox players celebrate the team's win in the 2005 World Series. It was 88 years after their last World Series win.

PERFECT

At one time, the White Sox were the most hated team in all of American sports. Now they are one of the most loved. They have continued their success following the 2005 World Series.

In 2009, Mark Buehrle became one of the few pitchers ever to throw a perfect game. This means not one player from the other team made it safely to first base. There had been only 17 other perfect games in the history of Major League Baseball. The White Sox themselves may not have a perfect history. Star players like Buehrle and Alexei Ramírez continue to make up for it, though.

Mark Buehrle threw his perfect game at U.S. Cellular Field on July 23, 2009. The White Sox beat the Tampa Bay Rays, 5–0.

CHICAGO WHITE SOX TIMELINE

1901

The White Sox play their first game in the new American League. They beat the Cleveland Blues.

1906

The White Sox beat the Chicago Cubs in the World Series.

1917

The White Sox win the World Series. They would not win it again until 2005.

1919

The White Sox lose the World Series on purpose. Eight of their best players are later banned from Major League Baseball.

1959

The White Sox become the American League champions but lose the World Series.

1956

Shortstop Luis Aparicio joins the White Sox. He will go on to become one of the team's biggest stars.

1991

The White Sox move into their new stadium. It will later be renamed U.S. Cellular Field.

2005

Ozzie Guillén leads the White Sox to win their first World Series in 88 years.

1994

A great White Sox season ends when Major League Baseball players go on strike.

GLOSSARY

CHAMPIONSHIPS (CHAM-pee-un-ships) Contests held to determine the best, or the winner.

DEFENSE (DEE-fents) When a team tries to stop the other team from scoring.

LEAGUE (LEEG) A group of sports teams.

LOGO (LOH-goh) A picture, words, or letters that stand for a team or company.

MAJOR LEAGUE BASEBALL (MAY-jur LEEG BAYS-bawl) The top group of baseball teams in the United States.

MANAGER (MA-nih-jer) The person in charge of the players and coaches on a baseball team.

PITCHING (PIH-ching) Throwing the ball for people to hit in baseball.

RIVALS (RY-vulz) Two people or groups who try to get or to do the same thing as one another.

SHORTSTOP (SHORT-stop) The baseball player who stands between second and third base.

SLUGGER (SLUH-ger) A baseball player who hits well.

STADIUM (STAY-dee-um) A place where sports are played.

STIRRUPS (STUR-ups) High socks that baseball players sometimes wear over their other socks.

STRIKE (STRYK) When people stop working because they object to something.

WORLD SERIES (WURLD SEER-eez) A group of games in which the two best baseball teams play against each other.

INDEX

WEB SITES

Due to the changing nature of Internet links, PowerKids Press has developed an online list of Web sites related to the subject of this book. This site is updated regularly. Please use this link to access the list:
www.powerkidslinks.com/agt/whitesox/